The Sylvester Stoddard tin shop and home.

NAUVOO

 The City Beautiful

John Telford

**EAGLE
GATE**

SALT LAKE CITY, UTAH

Library of Congress Cataloging-in-Publication Data

Telford, John, 1944-
    Nauvoo / John Telford.—Rev. ed.
      p.   cm.
    ISBN 1-57008-798-9 (alk. paper)
    1. Nauvoo (Ill.)—History.   2. Nauvoo (Ill.)—History—Pictorial works.   3. Historic buildings—Illinois—Nauvoo—Pictorial works.
4. Mormons—Illinois—Nauvoo—History.   5. Mormons—Illinois—Nauvoo—History—Pictorial works.   I. Title.
    F549.N37 T45 2002
    977.3'43—dc21
                                             2002004282

Printed in the United States of America   42316-6935
Inland Press, Menomonee Falls, WI

10 9 8 7 6 5 4 3 2 1

Before the spring of 1995, Nauvoo was a place I had only heard or read about as related to the history of The Church of Jesus Christ of Latter-day Saints. I knew the stories of the Saints who had lived there and of their forced exodus across the Mississippi River as they began their legendary trek west, but I had never been to Nauvoo. My sister and her husband, Cindy and Kim Averett, who were living in Lincoln, Nebraska, frequently described the city's beauty and the spirit that pervades this important Church historic site. Cindy kept saying to me, "You ought to do a book on Nauvoo."

I had been on the faculty of Brigham Young University for four years at that time. Having stood in awe of the creative work that several of my talented colleagues had done to support the Church, I made a commitment to myself to follow their example. A grant proposal through my college, Fine Arts and Communications, was accepted, allowing me one week in Nauvoo to produce enough photographs, both interior and exterior, to compile a book.

With high anticipation I called Cindy and Kim to set a date. And then a sense of panic came over me. Every other book I had done took years of work in the field. How could I possibly get all the photographs I needed in just six days? Would the light and weather cooperate? Could I get permission and cooperation from the authorities in Nauvoo? How would I find the time to scout the sites and do all the extensive setup and lighting for each

to the window of the motel to see if the moon was still in a clear sky. I nervously tried to visualize where the moon would be at sunrise. Finally, when the agreed-upon predawn hour arrived, we arose, knelt in prayer, and set out to begin the long-anticipated photographic work. The full moon was still bright in a sky that was beginning to take on hues of pink and purple. Experience had taught me that I had less than twenty minutes to find a site, set up the camera, calculate the settings, and begin making exposures. After looking at two or three possibilities, we decided on the Seventies Hall. Using the longest lens I had (450 mm) to keep the moon as large as possible in relation to the building, we set up in a field of dewy grass for the first of more than a hundred photographs.

We photographed each morning beginning at about 5:30, shooting until the "sweet light" around sunrise faded into ordinary daylight. Then we turned our attention to interior photographs. We worked inside until late afternoon, when the light was favorable for outside work again. Then we photographed outside until after sunset, about 9:30, after which we went home to prepare for the next day.

The third morning was overcast and rather ominous looking. Disappointment started to set in as I said to myself, "I have only six days to do all this work; I need every morning to be clear and beautiful." But we went out anyway to see what might present itself. I photographed a dramatic cloud-filled sky hanging over the Heber C. Kimball home. Later that day it started to rain. While I photographed the interior of the Wilford Woodruff home,

interior photograph? And on and on. Yet I knew from experience that I would just have to take one picture at a time and do the best I could with the conditions I found.

A full moon rose into a purple sky over the Mississippi River as Kim and I, accompanied by my wife, Valerie, crossed the bridge approaching Nauvoo. Just reading the sign announcing "Nauvoo, one mile" sent chills down my spine. "This is it," I thought. "This is where the Prophet Joseph Smith lived. This is where the Saints built the beautiful city." It was dark, but the light of the full moon made the sites readily recognizable. Seeing the Homestead, Brigham Young's home, Heber C. Kimball's home, and Parley Street running right into the Mississippi brought a flood of emotion.

I kept waking up during that first night and walking

the rain pounded down outside. Before it stopped, four inches had fallen.

The overcast sky the next morning tempted us to sleep in. But again I thought, "We have been presented with these conditions; let's go see what we can make of them." As we drove halfheartedly past the Red Brick Store, I felt compelled to get out of the car and take a look. I found myself walking into the trees, farther and farther away from Joseph's store, trying to step around the puddles that had collected from the previous night's rain. Then I turned around to see a scene of unexpected beauty: the reflection of the store in a large pool of rainwater. This was the store where the Relief Society was organized in March 1842, the store where the first temple endowment was given to members of the Twelve in May of that same year. A spiritual feeling came over me as I made several exposures and realized that the weather conditions were a gift.

During the week, several other picture opportunities presented themselves as I found myself being drawn to vantage points that were not typical for me. I realized that my prayers for guidance were being answered. In addition, the variety of weather provided much more diverse conditions than I could ever have hoped for.

I photographed the site where the temple had stood. I tried to visualize its size and magnificence. The missionaries at the site explained that it was about the same height as the water tower located just east of where the temple stood. "It was one of the most beautiful buildings in all of Illinois at the time," they said. I walked around the site, following the stones that marked the foundation. I could only imagine, with help from a small nearby replica, the Nauvoo Temple's scale and detail. I had to remind myself that as wonderful as the rest of Nauvoo was and is, the temple was the focus and the most important building in the city.

The walls of the temple, which the Prophet had seen in vision, were only half completed in June 1844 as the Prophet rode past them for the last time on his way to Carthage Jail. For the next two years, Brigham Young and the Quorum of the Twelve made completion of the Nauvoo Temple their highest priority. The temple is estimated to have cost more than a million dollars. Even at that, most of the labor to build it was donated by Church members.

Limestone was cut from a quarry just off Main Street near the Mississippi River. Wood was transported down the river on huge rafts from Wisconsin. A large bell weighing

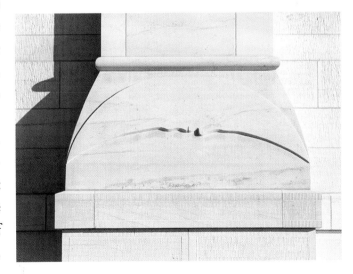

more than 1,500 pounds was contributed by British converts and mounted in the tower atop the temple. As I stood on the temple site, I tried to imagine the bell's silvery notes reverberating throughout Nauvoo along with shouts of "Hosanna to God and the Lamb" as the frenzy of temple work proceeded prior to the exodus.

As rooms were completed, they were dedicated and used for baptisms, endowments, and sealings. From mid-December 1845 to February 7, 1846, when the exodus began, more than 5,600 Saints received the blessings and ordinances of the temple. Several thousand Saints still lived in Nauvoo as of May 1, 1846, when Orson Hyde publicly dedicated the temple. Sometime during the following year the great bell was removed from the tower and transported by ox team to Utah. Within three years, the temple was gone, destroyed by fire and tornado.

As William Clayton wrote the words to "Come, Come, Ye Saints," he probably had in mind the blessings of the temple. He was on a cold muddy trail, slowly making his way across Iowa. He had just received word of the birth of his son back in Nauvoo. "And should we die before our journey's through, happy day! All is well!" The Saints had been endowed with power from on high. They had been sealed. Nothing could take those blessings away from them—not even death.

Because of the success of my first week in Nauvoo, my college grant was renewed, making it possible for me to return three more times during different seasons. The last of those trips fell on the weekend of the sesquicentennial commemoration of the Saints' exodus from the city.

Temperatures had dropped below zero, just as they had 150 years before. The Mississippi River was frozen solid, just as it was then. Despite the cold, I felt comfortable in a Nauvoo that is now familiar and full of friends.

In the closing session of the April 1999 general conference, President Gordon B. Hinckley made the surprising announcement that the Nauvoo Temple would be rebuilt. Two and a half years later, as construction was nearing completion, I was invited to photograph the placing of the angel Moroni on top of the temple. It was September 21, 2001, the anniversary of Moroni's first visit to Joseph in 1823.

A crowd of several hundred had gathered—small in comparison to the several thousand who attended the dedication in 1846 and smaller still in comparison to the hundreds of thousands at the open house and dedication of the new temple in May and June 2002. But anticipation and enthusiasm filled the air as the statue of Moroni was brought onto the temple grounds. It was placed at ground level for all to see, and crowds pressed close for a glimpse.

After more than an hour, the signal was given to hoist the angel to the top of the temple. An American flag had been attached to the cable just above the angel as a tribute to the thousands who had lost their lives during terrorist attacks in New York City, Washington, D.C., and Pennsylvania just ten days before, on September 11. On top of the temple tower, crews made last-minute preparations for the angel. In the belfry, electricians made final electrical connections for the bell.

The angel was lifted from the ground and flown in a wide arch from the north side of the temple, around to the west, and then to the south, flying higher and higher as it went. It finally rested atop the tower and belfry. Construction foremen made final adjustments and gave the signal of completion. A tremendous cheer filled the air from the crowds below. At that moment, the newly installed replica of the original Nauvoo Bell pealed forth its silvery chimes. For the first time in more than a century and a half, the ringing of the Nauvoo Bell reverberated up and down the Mississippi River.

In February 2002 I made one more trip to Nauvoo to photograph the temple as near to completion as the deadline for this book would allow. It was dark as Valerie and I drove into Nauvoo on Highway 96. As the temple—rising above the trees and the old water tower—came into view, Valerie gasped at the beauty of the glowing sight. Later, in speaking to several local residents, we learned that

the winter had been unusually warm, with no hard freezes so frequent in this part of the country. Work had continued uninterrupted, with light shining from the temple windows both day and night.

During the next few days, as I photographed the Nauvoo Temple from several different vantage points, I realized that it is once again the focal point of Nauvoo. For at least a mile up and down the Mississippi it can be seen rising above the trees as an alabaster beacon set on a hill. President Gordon B. Hinckley chose June 27, 2002, for the temple's dedication. The date is fitting, for it is the anniversary of Joseph and Hyrum's martyrdom. With a temple in its midst, the City of Joseph is once again the City Beautiful.

Day dawns on the Mississippi River, which was the lifeblood of Nauvoo. Not only did the river sustain commerce and encourage growth, "it assisted the gathering of the Saints and served as the baptismal font for hundreds at a time" (George W. Givens, Old Nauvoo *[Salt Lake City: Deseret Book, 1990], 32).*

Sunstones were placed atop each of
the thirty pilasters that formed the
exterior walls of the Nauvoo Temple.
This sunstone, located at the
Nauvoo Visitors Center, and two
others—one owned by a private
collector in Provo, Utah, and the
other held by the Smithsonian—are
believed to be the only existing
originals. The sunstones and
moonstones for the new Nauvoo
Illinois Temple were carved by State
Stone in Salt Lake City.

Left: Until the Nauvoo Temple
was built, no buildings in the city
could accommodate large gatherings
of Latter-day Saints. During the
summers, therefore, large groups
would gather in this grove west of
the temple and in the grove east
of the temple to hear the Prophet
Joseph Smith deliver some of his
most powerful discourses.

Several brick kilns in Nauvoo fired
thousands of bricks used in the
construction of homes, stores, and
other buildings.

*Joseph Smith's Red Brick Store was the
site of many important meetings,
including the organization of the Relief
Society on March 17, 1842. At this store
on February 20, 1844, the Prophet
"instructed the Twelve to send out a
delegation and investigate the locations of
California and Oregon and find a good
location where we can remove after the
Temple is completed and build a city in a
day and have a government of our own
in a healthy climate"* (Joseph Smith,
an American Prophet's Record: The
Diaries of Joseph Smith, *ed. Scott H.
Faulring [Salt Lake City: Bookcraft,
1954–56], 447).

The Homestead was Joseph Smith's first home in Nauvoo. The blockhouse portion was built before he arrived, but the Prophet added the kitchen and dining area (above), which was used for several months as an administrative office for the Church. The small log cabin in back of the home was used as a summer kitchen.

Left: This home, which Brigham Young completed in May 1843, was one of the few brick homes built in Nauvoo. "I . . . felt thankful to God for the privilege of having a comfortable, though small habitation," he wrote the day he moved in (Brigham Young, diary, 31 May 1843).

Above: In the council room of the Brigham Young home, Church leaders formulated plans for the Saints' exodus to the Rocky Mountains.

Wilford Woodruff completed his home in the fall of 1845, just sixty days before he fled from Nauvoo. He counted the 14,574 bricks used to construct his home, selecting the best ones for the home's front. This home was the first building in Nauvoo to be authentically restored (Sacred Places: Ohio and Illinois, *ed. LaMar C. Berrett [Salt Lake City: Deseret Book, 2002], 167).*

"My house has been a home and resting-place for thousands, and my family many times obliged to do without food, after having fed all they had to visitors," said the Prophet Joseph Smith of welcoming both the poor and the prosperous to the Mansion House. *"I have been reduced to the necessity of opening 'the Mansion' as a hotel"* (History of The Church of Jesus Christ of Latter-day Saints, *ed. B. H. Roberts, 2d ed. rev., 7 vols. [Salt Lake City: The Church of Jesus Christ of Latter-day Saints, 1932–51], 6:33*).

Right: When the Prophet moved his family into the Mansion House in 1842, the study area of the house became the administrative office for the Church. The Mansion House was also the site of Nauvoo's most celebrated parties.

Left: John Taylor's home was located between the post office and the Times and Seasons *and* Nauvoo Neighbor *printing office. This area of Main Street was a hub of activity in 1845 as construction of the Nauvoo Temple neared completion and the exodus of the Saints to the West approached.*

Above: The Saints carried this rocking horse, belonging to a son of John Taylor, from Nauvoo to Utah.

The Cheap Riser Boot Shop competed with about a dozen other cobblers in Nauvoo. George Riser made his shoes of rawhide, selling them at the "cheap" price of less than two dollars.

Right: The interior of the popular Scovil Bakery, where members of the Lucius Scovil family—who lived behind the bakery in a log cabin—baked breads, pies, cookies, cakes, and crackers.

Left: Heber C. Kimball's home, one of the most beautiful brick homes in Nauvoo, featured a large dining room and an ornate widow's walk.

Above: When it was time for Heber C. Kimball to leave his home, he said, "There may be individuals who will look at their pretty houses and gardens and say, 'it is hard to leave them'; but I tell you, when we start, you will put on your knapsacks, and follow after us" (Times and Seasons, *1 November 1845, 1012*).

The Windsor Lyon Drug and Variety Store offered a variety of merchandise, including dry goods, groceries, crockery, books, stationery, drugs, patent medicines, paints, dyes, boots, shoes, military goods, and home-grown herbs.

Inside the Times and Seasons *and* Nauvoo Neighbor *printing office, a galley of the* Nauvoo Neighbor *is prepared for printing using hand-set type. The* Times and Seasons, *published 1840–46, emphasized Church thought and doctrine, while the* Nauvoo Neighbor, *published 1843–45, was more of a secular publication.*

Right: The Cultural Hall, also known as the Masonic Hall, was the center of activity in Nauvoo. Here city residents attended a variety of religious and political meetings, concerts, dances, banquets, parties, and plays, featuring such local actors as Brigham Young (Sacred Places: Ohio and Illinois, *155–56*).

In the bricked area near the northeast cornerstone of the Nauvoo Temple was a grand circular staircase. The new temple has a circular staircase in the southwest corner.

Left: Stones from a limestone quarry, now under water, were hewn and then shaped to create the exterior façade of the Nauvoo Temple. Saints volunteered one day in ten to work in the quarry and haul limestone blocks to the temple site. The walls of the rebuilt temple have been faced with limestone quarried near Russelville, Alabama, which closely matches the original.

"I looked upon the Temple and City of Nauvoo as I retired from it and felt to ask the Lord to preserve it as a monument of the sacrifice of his Saints," Wilford Woodruff wrote (Wilford Woodruff's Journal: 1833–1898, *9 vols., ed. Scott G. Kenney [Midvale, Utah: Signature Books, 1983], 3:49).*

The Pendleton Schoolhouse consisted of a two-level blockhouse, where the family lived, and a lean-to connected to the back, where school was held.

Right: Lucy Mack Smith Home, where the Prophet's mother lived for a short time in 1846 with the family of her daughter Lucy (Sacred Places: Ohio and Illinois, *159*).

The main floor of the Seventies Hall housed a chapel built for thirty-four quorums of seventies. Offices for the seventies were located on the second floor.

Right: The sun sets over Seventies Hall, where many newly called missionaries practiced preaching before leaving for their assigned fields of labor.

The Carthage Jail was constructed of limestone in 1824. In 1844, only two rooms were used to detain prisoners; the jailer and his family resided in the remaining rooms.

Right: On the afternoon of June 27, 1844, the Prophet Joseph Smith, his brother Hyrum, Willard Richards, and John Taylor occupied this room when an armed mob surrounded the jail. The Prophet and his beloved brother were martyred in the ensuing attack, and Elder Taylor was seriously wounded.

The bodies of Joseph and Hyrum Smith have been exhumed and reinterred on three occasions. The current gravesite of Joseph, Hyrum, and Emma Smith is in a family cemetery next to the Homestead.

Right: The bodies of Joseph and Hyrum Smith were once secretly buried in the courtyard of the partially completed Nauvoo House.

Left: This statue of Joseph and Hyrum Smith, by Dee Jay Bawden, stands adjacent to the Carthage Jail, reminding visitors that "in life they were not divided, and in death they were not separated" (D&C 135:3).

The Nauvoo Temple can be seen up and down the Mississippi River for more than a mile in either direction—just as in 1846.

Limestone fragments and rubble from the original Nauvoo Temple can be seen today in many buildings throughout the city.

Left: Headstones dating from Nauvoo's early days are still prominent in the Old Nauvoo Burial Grounds.

Left: A replica of the original Nauvoo bell, cast by Petit Fritsen Bell Foundry in the Netherlands, began chiming from the temple belfry on September 21, 2001, after a statue of the angel Moroni was set in place on top of the temple. The date marked the anniversary of Moroni's first visit to the Prophet Joseph Smith in 1823.

Right: "In the afternoon, Elder William Weeks (whom I had employed as architect of the Temple) came in for instruction," the Prophet recorded. "I instructed him in relation to the circular windows designed to light the offices in the dead work of the arch between stories. He said that round windows in the broad side of a building were a violation of all the known rules of architecture, and contended that they should be semicircular—that the building was too low for round windows. I told him I would have the circles, if he had to make the Temple ten feet higher than it was originally calculated. . . . 'I wish you to carry out my designs. I have seen in vision the splendid appearance of that building illuminated, and will have it built according to the pattern shown me'" (History of the Church, 6:196–97).

Left: "*Public prejudice being so strong against us, and the excitement becoming alarming, we determined to continue the administration of the ordinances of the endowment night and day,*" wrote Brigham Young in January 1846 (History of the Church, 7:570). *By early spring 1846, approximately 5,600 Latter-day Saints had received their temple endowment.*

Right: "*One light at the centre of each circular window would be sufficient to light the whole room,*" *creating a "remarkably grand" effect, said the Prophet Joseph Smith* (History of the Church, 6:197).

Left: "The Spirit, Power, and Wisdom of God reigned continually in the Temple and all felt satisfied that during the two months we occupied it in the endowments of the Saints, we were amply paid for all our labors in building it," Erastus Snow recalled (Lisle G. Brown, "The Sacred Departments for Temple Work in Nauvoo: The Assembly Room and the Council Chamber," *BYU Studies* 19 [Spring 1979], 374).

Above: Round windows, all glazed with handblown glass, were made by a team of craftsmen from the Allyn Historic Sash Company of Nauvoo. The painting of 49,000 window-frame edges, which included 36,000 feet of putty, was done three times with no masking tape, razor blades, or cut lines (*Nauvoo Temple Times, February 2002, 2*).

Little is known of the original appearance of the temple's east façade. A journal entry by William Clayton and a single sketch by temple architect William Weeks were the basis for this design.

Left: Thirty sunstones grace the temple's exterior. Variations of the sunstone motif are seen throughout the interior of the temple as well. Starstones, located above each sunstone and featuring an elongated facet pointing downward, symbolize the morning star receiving its light from the sun.

While they toiled and sacrificed to build the Nauvoo Temple, many of the Saints lived in log cabins and blockhouses.

Right: In February 1846, in subzero temperatures, the first Saints left Nauvoo for the West. The last building they passed was the Seventies Hall.

"My last act in that precious spot was to tidy the rooms, sweep up the floor, and set the broom in its accustomed place behind the door," wrote Bathsheba Smith. *"Then with emotions in my heart . . . I gently closed the door and faced an unknown future, . . . faced it with faith in God and with no less assurance of the ultimate establishment of the Gospel in the West and of its true, enduring principles, than I had felt in those trying scenes in Missouri"* (Carol Cornwall Madsen, In Their Own Words: Women and the Story of Nauvoo *[Salt Lake City: Deseret Book, 1994], 213).*

Latter-day Saints began their exodus west by crossing the frozen Mississippi.

Right: Covered wagons at the end of Parley Street await the dawn of a chilly Nauvoo morning. Parley Street was nicknamed "Street of Tears" in memory of the sorrow of the exiled Saints as they waited their turn to cross the river and begin their trek west.

Left: The Nauvoo Temple was publicly dedicated from April 30 to May 3, 1846, more than five years after the cornerstones were laid on April 6, 1841. Construction of the Nauvoo Illinois Temple, which began with a groundbreaking and site-dedication ceremony on October 24, 1999, and ended with dedicatory ceremonies on June 27, 2002, took less than three years.

Right: The elliptical window at the top of the temple's east side, which provides light for the celestial room, is 21 ½ feet wide and 8 ¼ feet high and contains 234 diamond-shaped panes of handblown glass.